TRAVELS WITH ST. MARK:
GPS FOR THE JOURNEY

TRAVELS WITH ST. MARK

GPS for the Journey

A Pedagogical Aid

Eugene E. Lemcio

WIPF & STOCK · Eugene, Oregon

TRAVELS WITH ST. MARK: GPS FOR THE JOURNEY
A Pedagogical Aid

Copyright © 2012 Eugene E. Lemcio. All rights reserved. Except for brief quotations in critical publications or reviews, no part of this book may be reproduced in any manner without prior written permission from the publisher. Write: Permissions, Wipf and Stock Publishers, 199 W. 8th Ave., Suite 3, Eugene, OR 97401.

Wipf & Stock
An imprint of Wipf and Stock Publishers
199 W. 8th Ave., Suite 3
Eugene, OR 97401

www.wipfandstock.com

ISBN 13: 978-1-62032-331-1

Manufactured in the U.S.A.

Contents

Abbreviations vii
Definitions ix
Preface xi

1. Politics. Human and Divine in Daniel / 1
2. "Son of Man" in Daniel 7. Vision and Interpretation (Ancient and Modern) / 3
3. Interpretations of Daniel 7. Summary of Main Positions / 6
4. (The) Son of Man "Cluster" in Daniel 7 and Mark / 7
5. The Gospel Surveyed. "The Forest" / 9
6. Mark 1:1. The Gospel. Its Beginnings and Content / 11
7. Mark 1, Psalm 2, Isaiah 42 and 1 Kings 12. Servant-Sonship/-Kingship/-Messiahship / 13
8. Mark 1 and the Testament of Levi 18. Jesus' Baptism / 15
9. Kingdom(s) in Mark / 17
10. Jesus and Asclepios. Healers Extraordinaire / 19
11. Mark 3 and the Testament of Levi 18. The Exorcism of Unclean Spirits / 21
12. Mark 3:27. The Parable of the Strong and Stronger Man / 23
13. Mark 4:1–20. Structure (OT Models: Ezekiel 17 and Zechariah 4) / 24
14. Mark 4:10–12 and Isaiah 6:9–10. The Reason for Speaking in Parables / 25
15. Mark 2–4 and Isaiah 1–6. The Larger Context for Speaking in Parables / 27
16. Mark 4, 7, 8. Mysterious Teaching and Incomprehension / 28
17. Signs and Wonders: Elijah, Elisha, and Jesus / 29
18. Mark 8, 9, 10. Christology ("the Son of Man") and Discipleship / 30

Contents

19. The Son of Man "Shift" / 32
20. Mark 11:15–18. The Temple "Cleansing" / 33
21. Mark 12:1–12. The Parable of the Vintner and the Tenant Farmers / 35
22. Mark 12:31–33. Commands to Love God and Neighbor. The OT and Judaism / 38
23. Mark 13 and Isaiah 13. The Shaking of the Foundations / 40
24. Forgiveness ("Release") of Sins in Mark / 42
25. Mark 14:24. The Blood of the [New] Covenant / 44
26. Mark 14:24. What Kind of Sacrifice? (Exodus 12, 24, and Leviticus 16) / 45
27. Mark 14:24 and 10:45. The Death of Jesus—and His Life: Bonding and Release / 47
28. Mark 15:39. The Centurion's "Confession" / 48
29. Mark 15 and the Wisdom of Solomon 2. The Crucifixion. A Paradigm Regained / 50
30. Christologies (Explicit) Surveyed / 52
31. The Messianic (and Son of God) Secret in Mark / 58

Appendix / 61
Bibliography / 63

Abbreviations

AV	*Authorized Version*
BCE	Before the Common Era
BR	*Biblical Research*
C & D	Cartlidge & Dungan
CE	Common Era
ET	English Translation
HB	Hebrew Bible
JB	*Jerusalem Bible*
JTS	*Journal of Theological Studies*
KJV	*King James Version*
LXX	Septuagint of the Greek Old Testament (=OG)
MT	Masoretic Text of the Hebrew Bible
NEB	*New English Bible*
NETS	*New English Translation of the Septuagint*
NRSV	*New Revised Standard Version*
NT	New Testament
NTS	*New Testament Studies*
OG	Old Greek (=LXX)
OGI	*Orientis Graeci Inscriptiones Selectae*
OSB	*Orthodox Study Bible*
OT	Old Testament

Abbreviations

RSV	*Revised Standard Version*
SNTSMS	Society for New Testament Studies Monograph Series
TB	*Tyndale Bulletin*

Definitions

Apocrypha — Lit. "hidden" (either because special or suspect—depending on the user)

Deuterocanon — Lit. "second canon"—a term devised in the sixteenth century, and used largely by Protestant reformers to distinguish documents originally composed (it was thought) in Greek and therefore not (as) authoritative as the "protocanonicals," the sixty-six books then corresponding to the Hebrew canon finally delimited by Jews during the early centuries CE.

Gentile — from the Latin *Gentes* ("nations"); i.e., all the nations besides Israel, non-Jews

Protocanon — See "Deuterocanon," above.

Pseudepigrapha — Lit. "false ascription," a derogatory term applied to literature which, on other grounds, was regarded as falsely attributed to an ancient worthy

Synoptic — a "seeing together," the term being applied to the first three gospels whose authors, despite their differences, are distinct from the Gospel of John in content and manner of presentation

Preface

THE USE OF "GPS" (Global Positioning System) in the title is deliberate for at least two reasons. First, it alludes to a modern means of guidance by satellites and thereby becomes immediately recognizable in a technological age. Second, "maps" might inadvertently imply that I am providing a topographical guide to the places which Jesus visited and the routes that he took in getting from "A" to "B."

Nevertheless, "maps" (which I shall retain for internal use) will be helpful in a practical capacity since consulting them should lead to the primary way of relating to Jesus: "following after" rather than "believing in" (as is characteristic of the Fourth Gospel, but not the others). It may well be that the latter phrase was for the first three (Synoptic) evangelists more mental and/or stationary than active and behavioral.

As before (in *Navigating Revelation: Charts for the Voyage*), I invite the teacher and student-learner (the ancient meaning of the Greek and Latin behind "disciple") to join me in traversing the terrain of the text—this time narrative rather than visionary apocalyptic. The following maps are to be understood primarily as guides to teaching and studying—as means, not as ends. They are not the same as the journey itself, nor the purpose of it (just as the menu should not be confused with the meal). Neither do the maps traverse each section of the terrain. There is plenty of opportunity for the serious inquirer to draw the results of his/her own as exploration along main roads, side streets, and alternate routes continues. Put another way, the selection of passages and themes is meant to be *illustrative* and *paradigmatic* so that all, beginners and those more advanced, can use them as models in expanding the range of their individual itineraries.

Rather than providing a rigid structure for indoctrination and memorization, such tables (accompanied by statements and questions) should foster orderly and disciplined instruction and study. The displays are of two kinds: the majority provides data in categories that can be inferred because of their frequency or strategic character (the subjective nature of this judgment being reduced by evidence and argument).

Interspersed among these are charts that demonstrate systematic analysis (a taking apart) and synthesis (a putting together) by posing "investigative" questions long used in literature and journalism classes: Who? (Agent: initiator or recipient), What? (Action/Event), When? (Time), Where? (Place), How? (Means/Manner/Method/Instrument), How Far/Many/Much? (Scope/Quantity), What Kind? (Quality), Why? (Purpose/Cause), So What? (Significance), etc.

Using these categories enables analysis and synthesis to be *comprehensive* in that many aspects of a selected narrative can be covered. At the same time, they make it possible for one to detect that which *integrates* the parts. Approaching literature in this way assists students to develop skills in *comparison* (noting similarities) and *contrast* (seeing differences). Furthermore, applying such neutral classification helps to *increase objectivity* and to limit imposing agendas foreign to a text. No rigid sequence need be followed when employing the above. They can be freely reordered to achieve the greatest pedagogical effect.

However, it is generally good practice to get an idea of the entire context, to see the forest within which individual trees grow, and to survey the lay of the land. Besides providing a sense of the whole, from which to interpret the parts, the bird's-eye view enables one to get a feel for proportion—where the emphases lie, what weight is attributed to certain themes. As the narrative journey progresses, one can more easily determine where a turning point or parting of the ways occurs. The importance of this practice cannot be overrated—as the display and discussion in map 5 will show.

In addition to leading the reader in comparing and contrasting categories within the text itself (thereby allowing the Evangelist to speak on his own terms and in his own way—the main objective), I provide opportunities for readers to compare and contrast the Gospel with external sources—both canonical and extrabiblical. Examples of the former are of three kinds: (a) the Old Testament of the Jewish Scriptures acknowledged by Protestant Christians since the Reformation, (b) the Old Testament of the Roman Catholic and Eastern Orthodox communions, containing Deuterocanonical writings integrated within Christian Bibles since earliest times, and (c) the New Testament. "Extrabiblical sources," refers to writings of two kinds: (1) those which at least some Jews (and some Christians?) had at some point regarded as authoritative (such as the Testaments of the

Twelve Patriarchs) and (2) Greco-Roman texts (such as those inscriptions that attribute cures to the god, Asclepios). This is an attempt to provide for modern readers a sense of the literary environment that shaped the religious world of Jesus, Mark, and the earliest Christians.

So far as the remainder of the NT is concerned, I have studiously avoided harmonizing Mark with other authors. However, in the case of the two remaining Synoptic Gospels (and, in a few instances, John), some accounts of the same event or teaching are similar enough that the maps will do double and even triple duty in providing a framework on the basis of which one can subsequently study the others on their own. (John is different enough in both form and content that he requires separate attention.) Consequently, I have provided chapter and verse notations in parentheses under the relevant map titles.

As before, I begin with those calling attention to themes in Daniel that have made such a profound impact upon the Synoptic Gospel tradition (and upon Revelation, for that matter): politics (both human and divine) and the Son of Man—the latter being Jesus' exclusive self-designation and the former finding expression in "the Kingdom of God": the central subject of his preaching and teaching.

Once again, I have used the NRSV, except in those passages referring to the son of man figure in Daniel 7 (where I resort to the RSV). I did so principally because this translation has preserved the expression "son of man" rather than converting it to the generic "human" or "mortal." Although not a title *per se*, the term retains a certain formal quality, which NT writers exploit when they appropriate it. Such usage is obscured by the NRSV's otherwise welcome efforts to avoid gender specific translation. Because this tool is meant to engage students (and teachers!) with primary texts before they resort to secondary resources, I have minimized references to the latter in footnotes. Secondary works supporting direct study of primary materials are cited internally and listed in the bibliography.

Perhaps a final word is in order about the "order" of events in Mark's gospel, given that both teachers and students will encounter various literary patterns throughout the following maps. The subject is an ancient one, in our case going back to the earliest external evidence about the gospel. Whatever one may think about the accuracy of this account, the tradition is remarkably frank about the history of the gospel's reception in the ancient church. Although writing in mid-fourth century, Eusebius of Caesarea cites the comments of Bp. Papias of Hierapolis who, at the time (ca. 140 CE) would have been in his mid-80s. (See the full text in the appendix.) This means that his life had spanned the end of the first century and the beginning of the second.

Papias claims to repeat the comments of a certain "Elder," who himself had heard the apostle John. Apparently responding to criticism that Mark had not written his account "in order" (in chronological sequence), the bishop defends the Evangelist along two main lines: (1) Mark himself had not been a follower of Jesus—therefore, a witness neither to his deeds nor words. However, (2) he had followed Peter, who had been "there when it happened and ought to know." (Would anyone care to fault him?) And this original had not given Jesus' teachings in order (chronological sequence) but as demanded by the needs of the situation/or the requirements of form ["khreia" can be rendered in either way]. Mark's assignment had been to write down everything that he had remembered of Jesus' sayings.

This account of ancient Christian apologetic serves to remind modern teachers, students, and the general reader that there are various kinds of order, depending on what the user intends to achieve. Thus, chronological order is the province of historians, scientists, and police who want to establish a sequence of events—as they had happened. Rhetorical order arranges arguments and information to persuade and inspire. Pedagogy and study require presentation and mastery of a subject according to a certain orderliness—which may differ among teachers and learners, depending on personality and content. (However, getting oneself dressed demands a certain order of steps: socks (always) before shoes, etc.) Literary order may have several, simultaneous goals: providing a theological/christological point of view ("According to Mark"), conveying information, persuading, inspiring, and giving pleasure.

1. Politics. Human and Divine in Daniel

	1	2	3	4	5	6	7	8	9	10	11	12	Totals
Kingdom	3	10	3	11	7	7	9	1	3		6		62
King	17	43	29	15	17	26	3	5	2	4	23		184
Reign (vb.)							2	1	1				4
Authority			3	8	4	1	6						22
Power(ful)		1	2			1		1	2		3		9
Ruler	1	2	3	1						1			8
Throne			1	4			2						7
	21	56	41	39	28	35	23				32		

1. Because Daniel supplies so many of the key themes and terms in the Synoptic Gospels (and in Revelation, for that matter), I display the data and provide the following observations and questions. Although textual variants in some cases affect the numbers, they do not contradict the overwhelming preponderance of the figures above.

2. The best way to reduce (if not completely avoid) subjectivity about determining the dominant theme of any literary work is to apply the criterion of frequency. Which terms and synonyms occur in most instances, at certain concentrations, and at critical junctures? This display indicates how much political terminology (both separately and collectively) covers the text.

3. As a working definition, regard politics to be an understanding of power and as a strategy for distributing it in human community. In the Bible, there are only two alternatives: human politics and divine politics. The latter is summarized especially by a multiple refrain at 4:17, 25, and 32: "The Most High rules human kingdoms and gives them to whom he will" and, according to v. 17b, "sets over it the lowliest of human beings." According to the LXX of 4:28(31), Daniel tells King Nabouchodonosor, "The kingdom of Babylon has been taken away from you and is being given to another, a contemned [or "despised"] person in your house. Lo, I establish him over

your kingdom, and he will receive your authority and your glory and your luxury so that you may recognize that the God of heaven has authority in the kingdom of humans and he will give it to whomever he desires. Now, by sunrise, another king will rejoice in your house and will take your glory and your power and your authority" (NETS).

4. The numbers represent Greek terms as they occur in the LXX, the Bible most often cited and alluded to by the writers of the NT. A comparison with Semitic and English concordances does not materially affect the quantity and distribution of the terms. All such reference works testify to the heavily political context of the writer's various themes. The quantity and variety of instances for royal terminology are themselves impressive. Can there be any doubt that dominion and rule are dominant themes in this book?

5. Regard the throne as the "seat" of power from which kings rule. In the extended chapter 4 in the LXX of Daniel, the throne imagery is increased severalfold. This is more apparent in the NETS.

6. Perhaps the clearest definition of Israelite kingship (at least its ideal) is provided by Deut 17:14–20. Distinguish between negative and positive aspects of the job description. See also Psalm 72.

2. "Son of Man" in Daniel 7. Vision and Interpretation (Ancient and Modern)

Daniel 7: Vision	Explanation #1	Explanation #2	Explanation #3
3 Beasts (2-6)			
4th *Beast*	**4 Kings** (17)	**4th** *Beast* (19-20)	**4th Kingdom** (23)
10 horns			**10 Kings** (24)
11th *horn*		**11th** *horn*	**11th King**
speaking great things (8)			
*speak*ing great *words* (11)			*speak*s *words* (25)
			against Most High [MH]
		made war with & conquered SMH (21)	wore out SMH
			tried changing times & law
			temporarily victorious
Ancient of Days [AD] *judges* (9-10)		AD *judges* (22)	court *judges* (26)
one like a son of man (13)	Saints Most High [SMH] (18)	SMH	People of SMH (27)
given	*receive*	*possess*	*given*
dominion			dominion
glory			
kingship	**kingdom**	**kingdom**	**kingdom**
universal service			*universal service*
indestructible **king**ship			eternal **kingdom**

3

1. Because Jesus exclusively employs "the son of man" as a self-designation, and because the expression is derived principally from Daniel 7, it is necessary to examine the dynamics of the original usage.

2. The overall political emphasis displayed earlier in map 1 lies behind its particular manifestation in this chapter, as the bold font highlights.

3. Although vv. 1–14 present the vision proper, explanations 2 and 3 also contain expansions (additional details of the original vision).

4. John J. Collins summarizes three main views about the identity of the son of man figure and the Saints/Holy Ones of the Most High: (a) a collective symbol for loyal Israel under assault, (b) a human representative of these people, and (c) an angel (Michael?) at the head of a band of angels—both being the heavenly patrons of God's earthly people. See map 3 for a fuller treatment.

5. Although the MT enables one to read v. 27—and (c)—in this manner, the LXX prevents one from doing so for two reasons: angels are never referred to as "holy"; and v. 27 speaks of "the holy people of the Most High" rather than "the people of the Saints/Holy Ones of the Most High" (MT).

6. I have argued in *TB* that we will be distracted from the central point by focusing on the figure's *identity* (one of the above). Rather, the stress should be on the nature of his *human-like condition*—regardless of who he is/represents: an embattled but loyal Israel, or its lowly human representative, or a vulnerable member of the angelic order (or one from the lower ranks). For the sake of argument, work with "son of man" as an idiom for humanity in its frailty and vulnerability—the downside of human experience. See Bowker, Burkett, and Lemcio.

7. And one needs to give close attention to the dynamic aspects of the mini-drama (narrative *in nuce*) taking place (rather than focusing on the *denoument*): a kingdom was granted to one who had previously had none; glory was given to him who had been without it; authority was bestowed upon a "personage" who had lacked it.

8. This phenomenon belongs to the widespread biblical theme of reversal: God raises the lowly and brings down the high and mighty. (See for example, the Song of Hannah in 1 Sam 2:1–10 and the Song of Mary in Luke 1:51–53.) Daniel and the Synoptic Gospels (and Revelation, for that

matter) underscore the primarily political nature of that reversal, as the frequent terminology abundantly illustrates. At issue is, who rules (really) and how?

3. Interpretations of Daniel 7. Summary of Main Positions

	1	2	3
"[one] like a son of man" (vv. 13–14)	*collective* symbol Only: —suffering of a "frail human" —exalted, empowered in the vision Only	*individual* human (the Messiah?) —No suffering —exalted, empowered in heaven	angel (Michael?) —No suffering —exalted, empowered in heaven
"saints of the Most High" (vv. 15–27)	God's holy people —loyal —embattled by kings (=beasts) —to be exalted, empowered on earth	God's holy people —loyal —embattled by kings (=beasts) —to be exalted, empowered on earth	God's holy angels —loyal —embattled by demonic "beasts" —to be exalted, empowered in heaven —parallel holy, loyalists embattled by kings on earth

1. C. F. D. Moule is a representative of those holding number 1.

2. Representative of the inclination to blend all three (inferring a divine-human figure who is exalted after suffering) is Seyoon Kim.

3. John J. Collins (whose summary I have elaborated upon) and Christopher Rowland are supporters of view 3.

4. What happens when one focuses less on the *identity* of the figure and more on the *nature* of his humanity: its frailty, vulnerability?

4. (The) Son of Man "Cluster" in Daniel 7 and Mark

	1	2	3	4	5	6	7	8
Dan 7:13–14								
1. Son of Man		10, 28						31, 38
2. Kingdom	15		24	11, 26, 30, 33		23		
3. (King)						14, 22, 25–27		
4. Authority	22, 27	10	15			7		
5. Glory		12						

	8	9	10	11	12	13	14	15
Dan 7:13–14								
1. Son of Man	31, 38	9, 12b, 31	33–34, 45			26	61	
2. Kingdom		1, 47	14–15, 23–25	10	34	8	25	
3. (King)						9		2, 9, 12, 18, 26, 32
4. Authority				28–29, 33		34		
5. Glory	38		37			26		

1. Consult map 9 for distinctions within the kingdom language. See the auxiliary uses of "king" in chapters 6 and 15.

2. Although there is nothing equivalent in Mark to the clustering of the four terms within the space of two verses in Dan 7:13–14, nevertheless, the frequency and distribution of the terminology in Mark indicates a natural

association and "logic." Can there be any doubt about the profound impact of Daniel 7 upon Mark's gospel (and, indeed, the entire gospel tradition)?

3. Be sure to observe other aspects of the son of man Christology in maps 5, 18–19, and 30–31.

4. Is it a coincidence that all five terms appear in chapter 13—in the passage most like Daniel 7 in its eschatological content and imagery?

5. The Gospel Surveyed. "The Forest"

	Chapters 1–7	Chapters 8–16
1. Place	Mainly North (Galilee)	Mainly South (Judea & Jerusalem)
2. Central Topic	Kingdom of God (KG): near, like…	KG (ch. 13: future)
		Christology & discipleship (see #s 5 & 6, below)
3. Miracles	+	Last one in ch. 10
4. Exorcisms	+	Last one in ch. 9
5. Christology	Jesus: Son of Man (SM) as authority	Jesus: SM as suffering, death, resurrection, & return
	Son of God (power): demons silenced	
	Messiah (power): Peter et al. silenced (8)	
6. Discipleship	Entry (8)	Community life: Status/power (9, 10)
7. Audience	mostly public (to crowds)	mostly private (to disciples)
8. Religious leaders' opposition	INcreases	INcreases
9. Disciples' understanding	DEcreases	DEcreases

1. This is meant to be an overview: an attempt to see the forest as well as the trees, to get the lay of the land, to achieve a bird's-eye view.

2. The line dividing "Place" into North and South should not be understood rigidly. Chapters 8–10 are more like a transition between the two regions. The same might be said about other divisions, as well (including horizontal ones). Be prepared for overlap (sometimes obscured in the map).

3. In which half of the Gospel is (obvious) power concentrated? With which topic of teaching is it associated?

4. Which Christologies are associated with this power?

5. Which Christology covers both halves of the gospel?

6. Which Christology would more likely be regarded as narrative in nature—the one most connected with the activity of Jesus?

7. Which Christology is most closely related to discipleship? See map 18 for a more detailed analysis of these co-ordinate themes.

8. It is not evident from the map, but 80 percent of Mark is devoted to the ministry of Jesus prior to his arrest, trials, suffering, death, and resurrection. However, the dictum of Martin Kaehler, that "the Gospels are Passion Narratives with extended introductions,"[1] has obscured this datum for over a century. In admitted overstatement ("To state the matter somewhat provocatively . . ."), the author lamented that something so *theologically* weighty was being minimized by historians whose biographies of Jesus devoted a mere 20 percent to the text of the passion narratives [the proportion in Mark]. So, he maximized the latter by calling the preceding stories "introductions." Yet, Kaehler had to acknowledge their substantial presence with the word "extended." While it is true that nineteenth-century biographers of Jesus (the target of Kaehler's work) had overestimated the gospels' historical value, it is equally true that he himself had undervalued the theological significance of Jesus' life (perhaps because of his Lutheran preference for the Pauline gospel, as expressed in 1 Cor 15:1–7?).

9. For the classic study in English for the Son of Man Christology in this gospel, see Morna Hooker.

---

1. Kaehler, *So-Called Historical Jesus*, 80, n.11.

6. Mark 1:1. The Gospel: Its Beginnings and Content

	Isa 40:9–10	Isa 52:7	Jesus (Mark 1:14–15)	Paul (1 Cor 15:3–4)
Content	God comes with might	God-King-Salvation	Kingdom/-ship of God	Death for sins, burial, resurrection
	—his arm rules			

The Beginning

1. C. E. B. Cranfield has itemized ten interpretations regarding the precise beginning of the Good News.[2] The map suggests that, given the allusion to Isaiah 40, where "gospeling/goodnewsing" appears in the context of God's coming, saving, and ruling (vv. 5, 9–10), and backed by Isa 52:7 and Mark 1:14–15, "beginning" should refer either to the prophet's message or to Jesus' proclamation.

2. The question need not be settled here. However, one thing is clear according to the evangelist: it did not begin as late as the death, burial, and resurrection of Jesus—as it seems to do in 1 Corinthians 15.

3. But, even here, some interpreters suggest that "according to the Scriptures" locates the good news much earlier. If so, this point has often been lost on many Pauline interpreters. And it remains for them to account for the difference in content—perhaps by citing Scriptures such as the ones above.

4. The statement may also be doing double duty in providing an alternative (a politically sensitive one, at that) to the claim made by a resolution about Caesar Augustus (whose rule embraced the years 27 BCE to 14 CE), published by the provincial assembly of Asia during the middle of his reign:

---

2. Cranfield, *Gospel*, 34–35.

"the birthday of the God [i.e., Caesar] has been for the world the beginning of the gospel [*euangelion*] concerning him. . . ." See the larger context in C & D.[3] A fuller version appears in Kee[4]—the translation differing, but not at the relevant points. For the Greek, see Dittenberger.[5]

The Content

5. What is the content of Jesus' good news proclamation, according to 1:14–15? Where are kingship and good news linked? Reflect upon Isa 52:7 again. Is it surprising, given the Isaianic texts, that Jesus' message should be about the politics of God?

6. Might the above justify translating v. 1 as "The Beginning of the Good News *by* Jesus Christ" rather than "*about*" him (both allowed by Greek grammar)?

Implications

7. What are the implications for evangelism, Christian education, and worship if Gospel proclamation were to start where Isaiah and Jesus do—and with their subject matter?

---

3. Cartlidge and Dungan, *Documents*, 5–6.
4. Kee, *Origins*, 76.
5. Dittenberger, *Orientis*, sec. 458.

7. Mark 1, Psalm 2, Isaiah 42, and 1 Kings 12. Servant-Sonship/-Kingship/-Messiahship

(Matt 3:17; Luke 3:22; John 1:34)

	Mark 1:11	Ps 2:2, 6–7	Isa 42:1	1 Kgs 12:1–19
1. sonship	My son	My son (7)		[son]
2. Spirit	Spirit as a dove		Spirit	
3. pleasure	Well-pleased		Well-pleased	
4. service			Servant	Service: people & king
			accepted	Offered, rejected
5. king	[Jesus]	[David & successors]		Rehoboam
—anointed=messiah/christ		—anointed (2)		—ditto
—son of God		—ditto		—ditto

1. The voice that Jesus hears at his baptism is an echo of Ps 2:7 (to the king: "you are my son" and Isa 42:1: "my Servant, in whom I delight"). The king of Israel was the Lord's anointed (mashiakh=messiah, Christos=Christ. Cf. Ps 2:2).

2. By joining this Servant Song with the Psalm, Mark suggests that Jesus' role is being defined as that of the Servant-Son, the Servant-King, the Servant-Messiah/Christ.

3. This much can be found in the commentaries. However, I cannot help suspecting that the Rehoboam incident in 1 Kings 12 lies behind describing Jesus' role in these terms.

a. On that occasion, the heir to the throne meets with Jeroboam and all the assembly of Israel who had gathered at Shechem to acknowledge him as king. The people make their appeal (vv. 1–4): "'Your father made our yoke heavy. Now, therefore, lighten the hard service of your father Solomon and his heavy yoke that he placed on us, and we will serve you.'" (Every third month's labor had gone unpaid [5:13–14].) The elders counsel him (vv. 6–7): "'If you will be a servant to this people today and serve them, and speak good words to them when you answer them, then they will be your servants forever.'" The issue has to do with the exercise of power. Each party has its own kind: royal power (from above) and people power (from below). In power sharing, no one suffers any lack.

b. However, Rehoboam takes the counsel of the lads with whom he had grown up in the palace (vv. 10–11, 14): "'My father made your yolk heavy, but I will add to your yolk; my father disciplined you with whips, but I will discipline you with scorpions.'"

c. What is the result of this power grab? Ten northern tribes ("Israel") revolt, separating themselves from Benjamin and Judah and from the Davidic dynasty (v. 16). Power grabbed results in power lost. The king returns to his capital with less sovereignty than before. Over the succeeding decades and centuries, destabilization, internal weakness, civil war, and a divided nation make both the north, and later the south, easier pickings for external enemies—principally Assyria and Babylon. Both Israel and Judah will be destroyed, never again to exist as viable political entities.

d. It is this model of kingship that Jesus rejects. To begin with, it is God's kingdom, not his own. He is its herald (proclaimer) and its interpreter (teacher) via parables. "The kingdom of God is like this" ["not like that," by implication]. (See also the cosmic consequences that St. Paul (in Phil 2:5–11) attributes to Jesus' acceptance of an alternative way of being Lord.)

8. Mark 1 and the Testament of Levi 18. Jesus' Baptism

(Matt 3:13–17; Luke 3:21–22; John 1:31–34)

	T. Levi 18:6–9	Mark 1:9–11
1. **Who? (subject/source)**	Father: Abraham	God
2. **What?**	Baptism	Baptism
	—Heavens opened	—Heavens tearing apart
3. **for Whom? (object)**	Son: Isaac	Son: Jesus
4. **by Whom? (agent)**	Spirit of Sanctification	John Baptizer, Holy Spirit (HS)
5. **Why? (reason/cause)**	Identity declared	Identity declared
6. **How? (means)**	Voice	Voice, HS in form of dove
7. **Result**	Legacy of divine majesty	Jesus: baptizer with Spirit
8. **So what? (significance)**	Sin terminated	Servant-son-/-king-/-messiah
9. **When? (time)**	Future	Immediate past
10. **Where? (place)**	In the water	Coming from the Jordan R.

1. If the majority of scholars is correct in dating the composition of this document [not to be confused with the book of Leviticus] in the mid- to late-second century BCE,[6] then we have here evidence that some Jews expected a kind of "baptism" to take place in the future in connection with the coming of a royal priest (vv. 2–3). Consult map 11, analyzing chapter 3 for expectations about his binding of Beliar and the trampling of unclean spirits by his followers. In this kind of religious environment, what might Mark be claiming about Jesus?

---

6. For the text, see Kee, "Testament of Levi," 778, 794–95, and Kee, *Origins*, 178, or Charles, *Apocrypha*, 314–15.

2. See map 7 relating this scene to OT passages for an appreciation of the differences between the father-son relationship in items 1 and 3.

3. What are the identity and role (numbers 7–8) of each baptismal candidate?

4. Editors usually regard "in the water" (#10) as a later Christian interpolation made to conform the passage to the gospel's account. However, this may be too hasty a judgment. Mark reports the event as taking place as Jesus was "coming out of the water" (v. 10. See also Matt 3:16, where the vision and audition occurred after he had come out of it.).

5. Although the Jordan River might be in the mind of the Jewish author and his readers, it is made explicit in Mark—both to remind Jewish readers and to inform Gentile ones of this theological geography, where Israel had entered the land promised to Abraham and his descendents.

9. Kingdom(s) in Mark

	Past	Present	Future
1. **Satan's**		If divided (3:24a)	Cannot stand (3:24b)
2. **Human**			Half of Herod's to give (6:23)
3.			Of our father, David (11:10)
4.			In conflict (13:8)
5. **God's**	Has drawn near (1:15)		
6.		Mystery of (4:11)	
7.		As if planted, growth (4:26a)	Harvest (4:26b)
8.		Like smallest of seeds (4:30)	Like greatest of shrubs (4:33)
9.			Come in power (9:1)
10.			Enter one-eyed into (9:47)
11.		Of such [children] is (10:14)	
12.		Receive as child (10:15)	How hard for rich to enter (10:23, 24, 25)
13.		Not far from (12:34)	
14.			Drink again in (14:25)
15.			Nicodemus was expecting (15:23)

1. During the last half century or so, scholars have proposed a more dynamic than static understanding of this expression. Rather than thinking of God's kingdom in terms of place, boundaries, and structures, they have proposed alternative language: God's reign, rule, and government.

2. One could say without fear of contradiction that this dominant theme of Jesus' preaching, enactment, and teaching has its roots in the book of Daniel [See map 1.], although the subject itself is widespread throughout the Jewish Scriptures. And its political character cannot be denied; neither should it be ignored nor minimized. At stake is an understanding about the nature of power and its distribution within human community. One can do this either God's way or take the human route—with its oppressive and disastrous consequences. The author of Daniel looks forward to its eschatological manifestation, when all opposition will be eliminated. Jesus announces that that time has been fulfilled (1:14).

3. Also evident is the fact that little attention is paid to human kingdoms (either Israelite or Gentile).

4. By far, God's rule, and its various aspects, holds sway.

5. Numerically speaking, in which phase (past, present, or future) does the emphasis lie? Which is a close second?

6. How are they related? Is this an example of the already-not yet phenomenon?

7. What is the significance of Jesus' proclamation in 1:15, so far as timing is concerned?

8. What is the difference between the NRSV's "Has come near" and the RSV's "is at hand" (1:15)? The former better conveys the sense of the Greek.

9. Although God's rule is proclaimed (ch. 1), its mysterious reality needs to be explained—which Jesus is shown attempting in ch. 4. He does this by using analogies—specifically, parables: literally "putting alongside" a known experience or truth in order to illuminate an unknown or mysterious one. "The kingdom of God is as if/or like this . . ." (vv. 26–32). What is not often (if ever) pointed out is that the comparison implies a contrast: "not like that" [i.e., the view that the original listeners—and readers, then and now—are holding].

10. See maps 13–16, which attempt to elucidate the difficult matter of the parables' function (vv. 10–12).

10. Jesus and Asclepios. Healers Extraordinaire

	Jesus	Asclepios
1. What? (event)	Cure of illnesses	Cure of illnesses
	Exorcism of demons	
2. Conditions	None/once: faith (in God)	Some (pre- or post-)
3. Response(s)	Nothing tangible	Presents, inscriptions
4. To Whom? (object)	Praise to God	Praise to Asclepios
5. Where? (Place)	Anywhere (except Temple)	Temple of Asclepios
6. When? (Time)	Anytime (except at night)	At night
7. (Occasion)	Publicly (usu.), privately	Privately, during dream
8. (Ideology)	Kingdom of God	(Universal good)

1. Perhaps the most widely-known healer in the ancient world was the divine-man Asclepios. His activity is sometimes put forward by scholars as a model from which the gospel writers drew when portraying the role of Jesus as healer. However, such claims must be evaluated in terms of closer analysis, which the map above helps to conduct. These data hold true for healings in the other Gospels and for exorcisms in the Synoptics. (Not a single expulsion of demons occurs in the Fourth Gospel.) See C & D for the texts, which I have selected because these inscriptions clearly predate the gospels.[7] Kee provides a somewhat-expanded collection of the material, with variations in translation which, however, do not affect the point being made here.[8] Dittenberger's critical edition of the originals remains standard.

2. As always, the dating of such parallels must be attended to: as contemporary or earlier than the gospel accounts. This is where the instances collected by C & D (even in the latest edition of 1994) must be examined carefully. Few of their samples come with dates (even approximate ones).

---

7. Cartlidge and Dungan, *Documents*, 151–2.
8. Kee, *New Testament*, 144–6.

One would have to be able to rule out the possibility that examples from the Greco-Roman world might have been influenced by Gospel accounts.

3. A. E. Harvey has observed that, among healing accounts throughout the ancient world, it is Jesus who is reported in the Gospels to have performed the most cures among the paralyzed, blind, deaf, and mute.[9] In the Jewish world, no one has been reported as doing so. Thus, among his contemporaries, he was unique in this regard. As well, these four constitute most of the healings within the Gospels themselves. In the light of Isa 35:5–6, what might Jesus or the evangelist be implying with such a concentration of these particular miracles—especially if they had addressed congenital conditions, in some instances, at least?

4. While Jesus accepts the occasional expression of faith that he or God can perform the cure (categories 2 and 3), he never requires it as a precondition. The only exception is perhaps the father of the demon-possessed son at 9:23–24. (The demon-possessed are themselves incapable of such respsonsiveness.) And, in the Synoptics, faith is never *in* Jesus (as it is in the Fourth Gospel). Nor does Jesus ever expect thanks or require those healed to follow him as disciples. Only once (the case of blind Bartimaeus) is it said that a cured person followed Jesus—and that on his own initiative (10:52b). Although he declares that Bartimaeus' faith had been the means of restoring his sight (v. 52a), Jesus had not made it a condition. What do these phenomena imply, so far as the concept of grace is concerned?

5. Although Jesus is certainly the agent of these demonstrations of power, their source is always God, who is also the subject of praise given by the astonished onlookers. What is the case with Asclepios?

6. While the differences in most of the categories above are obvious, that of ideology (#8) is more subtle. One must look to texts such as 3:22–27 and 6:12–13 to make the distinction.

---

9. Harvey, *Jesus*, 115–17.

11. Mark 3 and the Testament of Levi 18. The Exorcism of Unclean Spirits

(Matt 10:1; 12:22–29; Luke 9:1–2; 11:14–20)

	T. Levi 18:10-12	Mark 3:13-15, 22-27
1. Who? (subject/source)	[God]	[God]
2. What? (event)	Binding (12)	Binding (27)
3. against Whom? (object)	Beliar	Strong man=Satan
4. by Whom? (agent)	Royal Priest/Son of Abraham	Stronger man=Jesus
	—empowered "children"	—the Twelve authorized (13–15)
5. for Whom? (object)	Possessed by evil spirits	Demon possessed
6. Why? (reason/cause)		Kingdoms in conflict (22–26)
7. How? (means)		By the word
8. Result	Evil spirits trampled	People freed
9. So what? (significance)	Paradise accessed (10–11)	God's Kingdom rules
10. When? (time)	future	Desert testing (1:13)
11. Where? (place)	?	[Judean] desert

1. See earlier comments on T. Levi in map 8 for Mark 1 and T. Levi 18: Jesus' Baptism.

2. The relevant portion of this text reads, "And Beliar shall be bound by Him, and He shall give power to His children to tread upon the evil spirits" (v. 12).[10]

---

10. See Charles, *Apocrypha*, 315 or Kee, "Testament," 795.

3. Of the four instances in the HB or in the Protestant OT (which, since the sixteenth century, corresponds to it), none portrays Satan as head of an army of demons opposing God and God's people. Nor are there any accounts of possession by unclean spirits—of the kind found in the Synoptic gospels and Acts. But they occur in the writings of the Deuterocanon (a more neutral term than "Apocrypha"), which are present in the LXX and Bibles of the ancient church, being recognized by Roman Catholic and Eastern Orthodox Christians since then. See especially Tob 3:17; 6:8, 14–15; and 8:3. See n. 1 of map 29 for the earlier and current situation among Protestant Bibles.

4. The view of Satan as head of an opposing kingdom occurs most frequently in books of the so-called "Pseudepigrapha" ("false inscription/attribution"), especially Jubilees and 1 Enoch. The latter, more prejudicial term (whether used by scholars or the dominant religious party) obscures the fact that at least some of this literature was regarded as authoritative revelation by the groups that preserved them. In the NT, Jude 14 (in another connection) cites 1 Enoch 1:9 as a prophecy uttered by the antediluvian ancestor.

5. Is it legitimate to conclude that Jesus, and at least some of his contemporaries, believed that these events were taking place during (and because of) his ministry?

6. If so, what may one conclude about the influence of this "intertestamental" literature upon the thinking of Jesus and Mark (along with the other Synoptic evangelists)?

12. Mark 3:27. The Parable of the Strong and Stronger Man

(Mark 3:13–15, 22–27; Matt 10:1; 12:22–29; Luke 9:1–2; 11:14–20)

(1) SATAN	(2) Strong Man	(3) Stronger Man	(4) JESUS
Controls demons	Controls house	Binds strong man	Exorcizes demons
Possess people	Keeps goods	Seizes goods	Frees People

1. According to the preceding context, Jesus is leading a war against the regime ruled by Satan. The kingdom of God that he had proclaimed in ch. 1 is being enacted in the exorcism of unclean spirits. This brief parable explains why he is able to do so.

2. It is the positive response in Jesus' defense against the accusation by religious leaders that he is both possessed by [the demon prince] Beelzebul and that he exorcises demons by him (3:22). Jesus had earlier raised a series of questions requiring a negative answer as to how this could be the case (vv. 23–26).

3. Where is the only other place prior to this verse where Satan has been encountered? How then does Jesus' brief comment elaborate what had occurred at the temptation, according to Mark?

4. At this point, recall T. Levi 18: "Beliar [another demonic leader] shall be bound by him."

5. At Rev 20:2, Satan is to be bound for 1,000 years. Amillennialist interpreters (who deny a literal period of 1,000 years at the end of history) regard this statement and Mark 3:27 as referring to the same event, but in differing genres/kinds of literature: historical narrative and apocalyptic vision.

13. Mark 4:1–20: Structure (OT Models: Ezekiel 17 and Zechariah 4)

	Mark 4	Ezekiel 17	Zechariah 4
1. Revelation	Soils Parable (3–9)	Parable: Eagles & Vine (2–10)	Vision: Olive Trees (1–3, 11)
2. Mystification	Incomprehension (10)	[Meaning unknown] (12a)	Incomprehension [3x]: (4, 12)
3. Rejoinder	"Do you not know?" (13)	"Did you not know?" (12a)	"Did you not know?" (5, 13)
4. Explanation	Parable explained (14–20)	Parable explained (12b–21)	Vision explained (14)

1. Although many (perhaps most) scholars regard this fourfold scheme as artificial, invented by the evangelist as part of his equally artificial secrecy theme, I have shown in a more technical study that it belongs to a pattern of teaching found in the OT (and later Jewish literature prior to or contemporaneous with the gospel).[11] The incomprehension in Ezek 17:12a (bracketed) is implied in the critical rejoinder.

2. In every instance, it is people "in the know" (those specially selected to receive the instruction) who fail to get the import of it.

3. If the form had become standardized by Mark's time, it nevertheless corresponds to the near-universal experience of both teachers and students—perhaps even among those using this book.

---

11. Lemcio, "External Evidence," 326–29.

14. Mark 4:10–12 and Isaiah 6:9–10. The Reason for Speaking in Parables

(Matt 13:1–23; Luke 8:4–18)

	Resistance	Consequence (1)	Consequence (2)
Isaiah	Rebellious Children (chs. 1–5)	Blindness/deafness (6:9–10)	No turning, healing but destruction (6:11–13)
	(Israel: elect, saved)		
Mark	Hostility to Jesus (chs. 2–3)	Blindness/deafness (4:11–12)	No pardon, forgiveness (3:29–30, 4:12)
	(by religious leaders)		"those outside" (3:29–30, 4:11)

1. It is no wonder that Christian preachers appealing for commitments to mission of one sort or another after reading the call of Isaiah stop at v. 8: "Then said I, 'Here am I send me!'" That which follows does not constitute an enviable assignment.

2. Not surprisingly, commentators go to extraordinary lengths to explain (away) the harshness of Jesus' (or Mark's) reply that the purpose of his parables was to blind and deafen and to harden hearts, thereby effectively cutting off the possibility of repentance. So, one reads that Mark mistranslated the original Aramaic, or that Mark's harsher theology needs to be distinguished from the historical Jesus' actual teaching, etc. However, if Mark 4 is read in the context of chs. 1–3 and Isaiah 6 is read in the context of chs. 1–5, then such drastic, desperate, and artificial moves are not needed. In both instances, the history of rebellion by God's people reaches a point of no return such that, the prophetic word, which would otherwise have stimulated spiritual sensitivity, becomes that which causes spiritual hardness—with its disastrous results.

3. To identify "those outside" contextually, relate what is said in v. 11 about no forgiveness to 3:29–30, where "never have forgiveness" provides a contextual link. What is the unpardonable sin? And who, according to the preceding context, has committed it?

15. Mark 2–4 and Isaiah 1–6. The Larger Context for Speaking in Parables

(Matt 13:1–23; Luke 8:4–18)

	Isaiah 1–(6)	Mark 1–(4)
1. Who? (subject/source)	God	God
2. What? (event)	Judgment	Judgment
3. Against Whom? (object)	People of Judah	"Those outside"
4. Why? (reason/cause)	Rebellion (1–5)	Opposition to Jesus (2–3)
5. by Whom? (agent)	Isaiah (6)	Jesus (4)
6. How? (means)	Proclamation (6:9–10)	Parables (vv. 10–12)
7. Result: deliberate (1)	Spiritual insensitivity	Spiritual insensitivity
	No turning or healing	No repentance/forgiveness
8. Result: deliberate (2)	Cities destroyed, fields burned	
9. So what? (significance)	Opportunity runs out	Opportunity runs out
10. When? (time)	Several centuries BCE	First century CE
11. Where? (place)	Judah	Galilee?

1. This display shows even more graphically how Mark appears to make parallel the situation in Isaiah's day—several centuries before—and Jesus' own experience.

2. Of course, in the latter, the circumstances are recounted in a more compressed manner. Jesus barely gets his ministry in Galilee underway before both religious and political leaders begin plotting his death (3:6). Later in the chapter, he is accused of being in league with unclean spirits in the very process of casting them out! Review maps 11 and 12.

16. Mark 4, 7, 8. Mysterious Teaching and Incomprehension

	Mark 4	Mark 7	Mark 8
1. Mysterious Teaching	Soils parable (3–9)	What defiles (14–15)	Leaven: Pharisees & Herod (15)
2. Incomprehension	Explanation requested (10)	Explanation requested (17)	Forgotten bread? (16)
3. Critical Rejoinder	No knowledge (13)	No understanding/ sight (18a)	No heart, eyes, ears (17–18)
4. Explanation	Parable explained (14–20)	Explanation given (18b–23)	Explanation given (19–21)

1. See map 13 for earlier scriptural models of this structural phenomenon in Mark.

2. What do you find in terms of the intensity of critical rejoinder (category #3) leveled at the disciples as the narrative proceeds?

3. Compare the criticism of ch. 8 with that of ch. 4 and the use made of the Isaiah 6 quotation (4:11–20 and 8:17–18). What does this tell you about the identity of "those outside"? Is it a static group? Note what is said about the blindness and deafness of the servant of the Lord himself in Isa 42:1–9 and esp. vv. 18–20!

17. Signs and Wonders: Elijah, Elisha, and Jesus

	Elijah	Elisha	Jesus
1. Nature miracle	1 Kgs 18:44–46		Storm calmed (4:35–41, 6:45–52)
2. Food multiplied		2 Kgs 4:42–44	Thousands fed (6:34–44, 8:1–9)
3. Sickness cured (leprosy)		2 Kgs 5:13–14	Leper cleansed (1:40–45)
4. Dead raised	1 Kgs 17:17–24	2 Kgs 4:32–37	Jairus' daughter raised (5:22–43)

1. Two extremes need to be avoided in general: claiming too much about Jesus and claiming too little about him.

2. Given the divinely endowed capacity of these prophets to perform such cures, is it legitimate to use them as proofs of Jesus' divinity?

3. Include in your reflection Jesus' warnings about the ability of false prophets to perform "signs and wonders" (Mark 13:22–23).

4. How, then, might it be said that Jesus' miracles functioned? Keep in mind Isa 35:5–6.

18. Mark 8, 9, 10. Christology ("the Son of Man") and Discipleship

s= suffering, d=death, r=resurrection

	Mark 8:31–38	**Mark 9:30–37**	**Mark 10:32–45**
Christology	Son of Man's s-d-r	Son of Man's s-d-r	Son of Man's s-d-r
Discipleship	entry	community	community
	self-denial	reversal of	reversal of
	cross bearing	power	power
	reversing values	status	status
			service: freeing up to do
			the bidding of an other

1. What might this pattern suggest, occurring as it does roughly midway in the gospel (see map 4)?

2. For a topic or theme to be repeated is a sign given by an author that it is important. Doing so three times in a biblical document carries special value since three (like seven) is a number for completion or perfection.

3. In this case (and recalling the contours of the broader christological "forest"), "the Son of Man" comes to the fore in these successive chapters.

4. So, what are the implications for the phenomenon that, following each statement of the Son of Man's suffering, death, and resurrection, teaching about discipleship follows?

5. What is it about the self (a creation of God) that needs denying (ch. 8)? Relate this to the fundamental temptation as recorded in Genesis 3. How does taking up one's cross differ from bearing life's burdens: ills, accidents, etc.?

6. What is being stressed in chapters 9 and 10? What are the implications for the fact that the topic continues to be the same?

7. What do you think is going on with the expansion of the theme in 10:42–45? What is the need which is being addressed with such a threefold and twofold emphasis?

8. Note the power terminology of 10:42–44 and the contrast with v. 45.

9. What does paying a ransom accomplish? How does this define service in 10:45?

10. In Greek, "kai," the word for "and" can (depending on the context) also mean "that is." Supply the latter in the blank between these statements: "the Son of Man came not to be served, but to serve":____ "to give his life as a means of release for the many." Is it legitimate to regard liberation as release for the purpose of serving the other?

19. The Son of Man "Shift"

(1)	(2)	(3)	(4)
8:30–31	9:7, 9	13:21–22, 26	14:61–62
Peter: "The Christ"	God: "My Beloved Son"	False christs: "I am he"	High Priest: "Christ, Son of the Blessed One"
The Son of Man: s-d-r	The Son of Man is to be raised	The Son of Man coming on clouds	The Son of Man: sitting ... coming

Here is another way of demonstrating Jesus'/Mark's preference for this term (not just statistically and by distribution) above the others.

1. Jesus is the only one ever to use it throughout all of the gospels.

2. It is the only expression that covers all aspects of his career.

3. It is the action term. The others are acclamations/confessions, saying more about his identity/status than his role/assignment.

4. It is the first and last self-referential Christology that Mark uses (2:10 and 14:62, respectively).

5. The first of the shifts (1) occurs at a crucial turning point in the narrative: Jesus begins to teach about the Son of Man's suffering, death, and resurrection. The final one (4) seals his judgment.

6. It is not the case that Jesus denies the truth of the acclamations; rather, he wants to qualify or interpret them. Alone, they appear inadequate or are perhaps liable to misconception.

20. Mark 11:15–18. The Temple "Cleansing"

(Matt 21:12–13; Luke 19:45–46; John 12:13–17)

Lev 12:1–(8)	1 Kgs 8:41–43	Prophets	Mark 11:15–17
			Money changers
Pigeons for poor			Pigeon sellers
	Foreigner prays towards	House→prayer→nations (Isa 56:6–7)	House→prayer→nations
		den of robbers (Jer 7:11)	Den of robbers

1. It is a scene that makers of movies about the life of Jesus love to film. For once, the mild-mannered, gentle Jesus of popular and Christian fantasy exhibits some emotion—gets angry. However, the point of this passionate demonstration in the temple is lost. So, the specific actions and statements of Jesus require closer attention.

2. As is often pointed out, moneychangers provided an important function. Pilgrims from the Jewish diaspora would have carried currency bearing the stamp of a Roman emperor on one side and a scene from Greco-Roman myth on the other. Such violations of the second commandment could not be brought into the sacred precincts. So, temple money was needed.

3. Thus, at one level, Jewish leaders were holding fast to the revelation of God through Moses, as expressed in the second commandment forbidding the making of graven images. However, they were missing the mark so far as other expressions of the divine will were concerned.

a. Thus, the reference to stealing ("cave of robbers," echoing the words of Jeremiah) needs to be associated with Jesus' overturning the tables of those who sold doves—which ought to have been priced low enough for the poor to afford when bringing sons to be circumcised and mothers ritually purified. By implication, Jesus (in classic prophetic fashion) accuses the sellers of overcharging the poor for the very occasion when the physical sign of Israel's covenant relation to God would be carried out.

b. Furthermore, when Solomon dedicated the temple, he prayed that foreigners would have access to pray alongside the native Israelites (a theme reinforced by Isaiah). However, in Jesus' day, they had been denied it. Our Lord thus attempts to restore the original purpose for the place where (as the king had confessed and prophet had predicted), the God whom the heavens cannot contain was pleased to focus his presence so that one and all could have access.

21. Mark 12:1–12. The Parable of the Vintner and the Tenant Farmers

(Matt 21:33–46; Luke 20:9–19)

Man/Lord (1, 9)	God
Vineyard (1)	Israel: nation/people
Farmers	Leaders appointed
Left long time	Responsibility handed over
Servants (2–5)	Prophets
Receive the fruit of the vineyard (2)	Mission identified
Beloved Son (the heir) sent (6)	Jesus
(Receive fruit from vineyard)	Mission identified
Respect/honor him	Response to God: possible-expected
Inheritance ours, kill him (7–8)	Reason for resisting Jesus
Cast him out and killed —nothing achieved (8)	Jesus crucified
Destroy farmers (9)	Jerusalem hierarchy destroyed
Give vineyard to others (9)	Change of leadership (to Jesus' followers: all Jews)
Rejected Stone→Corner Stone (10–11)	Reversal: resurrection and supremacy

1. This (and the Synoptic parallels) is the only passage that provides Jesus' perspective on the entire story of God's relationship with God's people (not an individual's story) and includes Jesus' own career. See Isaiah 5 for the image of Israel as a vine(yard).

2. It represents the only time in the Synoptic gospels were Jesus uses "son" publicly in such a manner. At most, the term functions as an indirect self-reference (in keeping with the parabolic mode).

3. What was the owner's purpose in sending the series of servants?

4. Did the owner expect the farmers' response to be positive—that is, *could* they have responded appropriately?

5. What was the son's mission? Would it have been needed had the servants succeeded?

6. Was the son's mission intended to be successful—that is, *could* they have responded in the appropriate manner?

7. Did the owner/father expect the response towards his son to be positive?

8. Did the father send the son to die? Was the son's death effective in any way—that is, did it achieve anything?

9. Did the father reverse the son's death—even though the rejected stone's outcome suggests it?

10. Is anything more than a change in leadership envisioned? Is any non-Jewish group to be constituted as "new" Israel—which would require a new vineyard? Or, can the account be understood as occurring within Judaism? Of what ethnic background were the original Christians and their leaders?

11. Why, then, did Jesus say in chapters 8, 9, and 10 that it was necessary (*dei*) for the son of man to suffer, die, and be raised? My own inference in the light of Mark 12 is that Jesus eventually came to the conclusion that the original intention of the mission would not succeed. The opposition that he had encountered from the leaders in Galilee would be paralleled and magnified in Jerusalem. Otherwise, one cannot offer a plausible explanation of why it was that Jesus did not publicly teach about either the fact or significance of his death. To the claim that doing so would have met with

confusion, one could reply that Jesus could have taken pains to explain it with parables, as he did with his mysterious kingdom teaching.

12. For the most comprehensive treatment of this parable to date, see *The Parable of the Wicked Tenants* by Snodgrass who, in a personal communication, cites M. Tolbert's *Sowing the Gospel* (pgs. 121–26, 231–39) as a prime example of interpreting the passage within the context of the entire narrative.

22. Mark 12:31–33. Commands to Love God and Neighbor. The OT and Judaism

(Matt 22:34–30; Luke 10:25–28)

	Moses (HB)	Moses (LXX)	T. Dan 5:3	T. Issachar	Jesus
Love God	Deut 6:4–5	+	Love the Lord	Love the Lord (5:2)	+
	—with all your heart				—all your heart
		—your mind			—mind
	—soul	—your soul			—soul
	—might	—your power		—all my strength (7:6)	—strength
			—all your life		
Love Neighbor	Lev 19:18	+	one another	+ (5:2), every human	+
	—as yourself	—as yourself	—with a true heart	—as my children (7:6)	—as yourself

1. This map shows what is often observed: that the two commands originated separately in the fifth and third books of Moses (who is speaking on God's behalf in both texts).

2. The word for "heart" in Hebrew refers to several aspects of human personhood. The LXX (not surprisingly) makes the point that loving God must engage the mind.

3. If the Testaments predate Jesus, then the two commands were apparently joined by the Jewish author(s). See Kee or Charles.[12] Who brings them together in the Lukan account at 10:27?

4. So, what is distinctive about Jesus' formulation in Mark?

5. There is no parallel to the scribe's subordination of "all whole burnt offerings and sacrifices" to love in these two dimensions (vv. 32–33). Jesus commends the ability to extrapolate his own teaching on this subject.

6. What is the relationship between love in these two dimensions and the kingdom of God? See map 9.

7. Although labeled by scholars as "Pseudepigrapha" [books with "false titles"], Jubilees (along with 1 Enoch) are regarded as canonical by the Ethiopic Orthodox Church, being placed between Deuteronomy and Joshua. (St. Jude at vv. 14–15 of his letter seems to have regarded 1 Enoch as scriptural, given his citing of 1:9 as a prophecy by the antediluvian ancestor.) A version of the two commands appears at Jub 20:2, 7.[13] In its widest sense, "pseudepigrapha" for some specialists would cover at least some of the writings designated as "apocrypha."

8. For my fuller study of the Synoptic parallels within the context of Second Temple Judaism, see Lemcio and Wall.[14]

---

12. Kee, "Testament," 803–4, 809; Charles, *Apocrypha*, 327–8, 334.
13. Charles, *Apocrypha*, 42.
14. Lemcio and Wall, *New Testament as Canon*, 67–77.

23. Mark 13 and Isaiah 13.
The Shaking of the Foundations

(Matt 21:1–8; Luke 21:5–11)

	ISAIAH 13	MARK 13
City	Babylon (1)	Jerusalem, Temple (1–2)
Occasion	Day of Lord (6, 9)	Son of Man coming in power & glory (26)
Political upheaval	**kingdoms, nations** gathering (4)	wars & rumors (7), **nation vs. nation, kingdom vs. kingdom** (8)
Human suffering	Pangs, agony, anguish—as a **woman** in labor (8)	Dreadful for pregnant and nursing **women** (17), days of distress (18, 24)
Cosmic disruption	constellations *not give light;* sun dark…moon not *shed* light stars *not give light* (10) heavens tremble, earth *shaken* (13)	sun dark*ened,* moon not *give* light (24) stars *fall from sky* (25) earth*quakes* (8)
Earthly agents	Medes (17) vs. Babylonians	kingdom vs. kingdom, nation vs. nation (8)
City	Babylon (19)	See above. [Judea (14)]

1. Note that Isaiah 13 speaks of an historical event: the destruction of Babylon by the Medes (vv. 1, 17, 19). Did the cosmic disruption (vv. 10–13) actually occur on this occasion? If not, might this be a dramatic way of saying that the destruction is to be thorough, that Babylon does not have a chance, that "heaven itself" will fight against it?

2. Are the same sensibilities to be applied to our reading of Mark 13? Did the phenomena of vv. 8, 24–25 occur when Jerusalem was destroyed in 70

CE? Do we insist that they must occur in the future? Is this a use of eschatological language to speak of historical events?[15]

3. It is important to interpret v. 26 in the light of Dan 7:13–14. First, is there anything in ch. 13 that demands a *downward* movement of the Son of Man? What is the direction in Daniel? Continue asking the question, "What did Daniel and Jesus see? Was it a direct perception of reality or did they envision a mediating set of symbols?"

4. Note that the Son does not know the day or hour of his return (vv. 32–33). Can his followers achieve a better, more specific knowledge of them than him? So, what about those efforts by prophecy gurus who engage in elaborate attempts to do that which Jesus forbade?

---

15. See especially, Caird, "Language," 219–71.

24. Forgiveness ("Release") of Sins in Mark

	"Forgiveness/Release" (noun)	"To Forgive/Release" (verb forms)
Jesus		by the Son of Man's authority (2:10)
God		
—implied	1:4, 3:29	3:28, 4:12
—explicit		2:7, 11:25–26
Disciples		11:25–26
—others		

1. The dynamics of forgiveness are much discussed; but neither the discussion nor an analysis of the English word itself provides a ready definition. However, the meaning of the Greek as the normal expression for "release/let go/dismiss" might help. In contemporary usage, one often hears this admonition to a person obsessing over a hurt or injury of some kind (usually interpersonal): "You have to let it go!"

2. Are you surprised that, on only one occasion is Jesus reported to have forgiven/released people from their sins, according to this—the earliest—gospel (2:5, 9–10)? Does this mean that forgiveness was not a condition for discipleship?

3. It was done by his spoken word and reported early in the narrative—not by his sacrificial death at the end of the story.

4. Who, then, is the primary agent of forgiveness/release, both explicit and implied?

5. Although the paralytic and his friends express faith that Jesus could heal him, did he require it as a precondition—either for the cure or for the forgiveness/release? Does this correspond to the concept of grace?

6. For an understanding of how the Markan Jesus regarded the significance of his death, see maps 25–27.

7. Does the rarity of the role of forgiveness in this (and the other gospels) suggest that, important as the need for and experience of forgiveness/release is, it was not the dominant purpose of Jesus' mission—as is often stressed?

25. Mark 14:24. The Blood of the [New] Covenant

(Matt 26:28; Luke 22:20)

	Exod 24:1–7 (Original Covenant)	Mark 14:24 ([New] Covenant)
Priest	Moses	Jesus
Sacrificial Victim(s)	oxen	Jesus
Bonding (scope)	God & Israel	God, 12 Disciples, & Others

1. Exodus 24 is the only place where "covenant" and "blood" appear together. So, this is the one that Jesus refers to when he speaks of a particular ("the") covenant. What was achieved by it? (See the next map also.)

2. I put "new" in brackets because the "better" manuscripts do not have the word. Editors suspect that scribes wanted to harmonize the accounts (including St. Paul's in 1 Cor 11:25) across the board.

3. However, what was implicitly new about it, given the display above? Although the categories are the same, what is different?

4. Jesus speaks about the significance of his death in only two places (and both are in private). Why is there no public teaching or even specific mention of it? (See the next map.)

26. Mark 14:24. What Kind of Sacrifice? (Exodus 12, 24, and Leviticus 16)

	PASSOVER (Exodus 12)	**SINAI COVENANT** (Exod 24:1–8) (see Jer 31:31–34)	DAY OF ATONEMENT *(Leviticus 16)*
Animal Sacrifice	lamb(s)	ox(en)	*2 goats* *—slain* *—freed ("scapegoat")*
Purpose/ Result	protection→ liberation of the **community** from Egyptian slavery	sealing / bonding of the **community**	*release from the* community's *sins by* the live *animal*
Date/Time	spring	no annual observance	*late summer or early fall*

1. The blood sacrifices of three different animals achieved different results at different times of the year.

2. Sacrifices were for those who were *already* God's people, called by him into special relationship as early as Genesis 12. They were not initiatory rites.

3. The Passover sacrifice was not for the forgiveness of sins, nor was covenant bonding. The former celebrated the *community's* freedom from Egypt so that Israel as a *people* could be joined by covenant to God.

4. Sacrifices on the Day of Atonement did not *get* Israelites "saved"; they *kept* them "saved"—salvation not understood as going to heaven and avoiding hell.

5. Jesus did not die on the Day of Atonement (which was almost six months separate from Passover). And Passover was not an occasion for achieving forgiveness.

6. Only the first two columns, "Passover" and "Covenant," are relevant to the Last Supper accounts.

27. Mark 14:24 and 10:45.
The Death of Jesus—and His Life:
Bonding and Release

	Life	Death
Release/liberation		Ransom (10:45)
Bonding		Covenant (14:24)

1. Please read in connection with maps 24–26.

2. Jesus speaks about the significance of his death in only two places—and both being in private to his disciples. Nothing is ever explicitly taught or said about it in public.

3. Presuming continuity between the life and death of Jesus, and using his own actions and words to interpret the meaning of his death, list all of those things about Jesus' life that brought release (the result of ransoming) and bonding (the basic idea behind establishing a covenant).

4. Note that the Greek translated "forgive" is the normal word for "release" or "let go." Apply this definition to the cures, exorcisms, resuscitation, teaching about law and tradition, etc.

5. Would it be fair to say that the Markan Jesus brought comprehensive release and bonding, both throughout his life and by his death?

28. Mark 15:39. The Centurion's "Confession"

(Matt 27:54; Luke 23:47)

Translation	Rendering	Greek Grammar
1. KJV (=AV) et al.	"the Son of God"	Permitted ("Colwell's Rule")
2. Jehovah's Witnesses	"a son of God"	Permitted
3. NEB	"God's Son"	Permitted

1. The KJV and others reflect the possibility that Mark intended an irony here: a Gentile foreigner and member of the occupying army's execution squad is able to recognize Jesus' identity/significance while his own people cannot. Another paradox is that Jesus is recognized by this high title at the lowest level of his career. Or is Jesus' "low" the new "high"?

2. "Colwell's Rule" says that, if a form of the verb "to be" follows the predicate nominative, the latter can be regarded as definite—other contextual elements permitting.[16] Here is the statement, according to the Greek order: "Truly this man [subject] son of God [predicate nominative] was [past of 'to be']."

3. Others besides Jehovah's Witnesses could advocate (or at least, tolerate) the anarthrous rendition, suggesting that Mark relates the level of understanding shown by a pagan foreigner, within whose culture great men were ascribed divine qualities, if not status, during their lives or in connection with their death. Consult C & D on this subject.[17] If among these personages was Caesar himself, is there a suggestion that this officer is switching allegiances—from one emperor to another?

4. The NEB reflects a mediating position.

---

16. Moule, *Idiom Book*, 115–6.
17. Cartlidge and Dungan, *Documents*, 199–200.

5. The main point is that evidence for Jesus' status neither stands nor falls on the translation of a single utterance. All the data from the Gospels, and the church's reflection upon them, were taken into account when hammering out Christian doctrine.

29. Mark 15 and the Wisdom of Solomon 2. The Crucifixion. A Paradigm Regained

	Wis 2:12–20	Mark 15:27–39// Matt 27:38–54	Luke 23:35–47
1. Who? (subject/source)	unknown figure	Jesus	ditto
2. What? (event)	ridicule at abusive event	ridicule at crucifixion	ditto
3. for Whom? (object)	[Jewish readers]	[Gentile Christian readers]	[ditto]
4. against Whom? (object)	"righteous man is God's Son" (18)	"This man was God's Son." (Mark 15:39//Matt 27:54)	"This man was righteous." (47)
5. by Whom? (agent)	hedonist, Lawless ungodly	Gentile Roman centurion	ditto
6. Why? (reason/cause)	threat to way of life	threat: religious & political	ditto
7. How? (means)	verbal & physical attack	condemnation by authorities	ditto
8. Result	insult, torture, death intended	death	death
9. So what? (significance)	a known paradigm	known paradigm embodied	ditto
10. When? (time)	unspecified	Passover	ditto
11. Where? (place)	unspecified	Jerusalem—Calvary	ditto

1. For almost 2000 years, the Wisdom of Solomon, along with other Deuterocanonical writings, have been integrated in Bibles of the Roman Catholic and Eastern Orthodox Churches. Protestant reformers in the sixteenth century broke with this tradition by segregating these books between the

OT protocanonical writings and the books of the NT, labeling the former with the pejorative connotation, "Apocrypha" [lit. "hidden things"]. From this point on among Protestant denominations, they functioned at best as historical resources for the "intertestamental" period (roughly four centuries) and as nonbinding guides to pious living, but not for doctrine. Early in the nineteenth century, Protestant publishers excluded them altogether. When ecumenical winds started blowing in the 1960s, versions of the Bible containing the Deuterocanon began being made generally accessible for a Protestant readership—as in the case of the RSV, NEB, and now NRSV.

2. Thus, the motif of a pious figure who suffers such physical abuse and scorn chronologically precedes the Synoptic Gospel accounts and links the verbal abuse at Jesus' crucifixion with the phenomenon of reproach against God's agent. In the Gospel of Mark, Jesus is faced with the contradiction that, as God's messiah/Christ, he ought to count on divine aid (or save himself—just as he had others). We can see the links between kingship, messiahship, and sonship in the Jewish Scriptures (map 7, notes 1–2 and map 30, notes 2 and 7). And Ps 72:1–7 (=LXX Psalm 71) makes much of the role of the king as the champion of justice/righteousness, particularly on behalf of the poor and those of low estate.

3. In Wisdom 2 (categories 4–5), the figure is charged with calling himself "the child [OSB]/servant of the Lord" (13) [*pais*, not *doulos*] and is accused of calling God his Father (16). Neither appellation comes to the fore in Mark before this occasion. Only in the garden of Gethsemane, just before his arrest, does Jesus address God in this manner (14:36).

4. With great irony, Mark turns this accusation by the leaders of Jesus' own people into an affirmation by the Gentile executioner.

5. One of the values of relating the Wisdom of Solomon to this scene in the Gospels is that it may help to explain why Luke and the other Synoptics differ at the point of the centurion's confession: the "righteous/just person" and "son of God" belonged within the same theological environment, being virtual equivalents. The third evangelist chose one of them, and the others the alternative. Thus, Luke's is not lesser or more historical. Nor did the other Gospel writers choose the higher of the two.

30. Christologies (Explicit) Surveyed

s=Suffering, d=Death, r=Resurrection, c=Coming

	The Son (of God)	The Son of Man	The Christ/ Messiah	Lord	Teacher/ Rabbi
1	[title (1)]		title (1)	God (3)	
	divine: my Beloved (11)				
	demon: Holy One of G. (24)				
2		authority to forgive (10)			
		Lord of Sabbath (28)		of the Sabbath (28)	
3	demon: SG (11)				
4					(38)
5	demon: S Most High G (7)			God (19)	(35)
7				="Sir" (28)	
8		sdr (31)	Peter: you are (29)		
		ashamed, comes (38)			
9	divine: my Beloved (7)	raised from dead (9)			(5, 17, 38)
		rejected (12b)			
		sdr (31)			

	The Son (of God)	The Son of Man	The Christ/Messiah	Lord	Teacher/Rabbi
10		sdr (33–34)	[Son of David (47–48)]		(17, 20, 35, 51)
		to serve, to give life (45)			
11				Jesus (3)	(21)
				God (9)	
12	owner: sent a beloved (6)			owner (9)	(14, 19, 32)
				God (11, 29, 30)	
			C.=the S of David? (35)	C. David's L. (36–37)	
13	nor the (24)	coming on clouds (26)	false C's. come (23)	God (20)	(1)
				of the house (35)	
14	HP: of the Blessed? (61)	seated, coming (61)	High Priest: the C.? (61)		(14, 45)
15	centurion: God's (39)		[King of the Jews (2, 9, 12, 18, 26)]		
			C., King of Israel (32)		

1. Although scholars have correctly stressed the need to investigate the "implied" Christology of the gospel(s), there is no warrant for ignoring the explicit expressions used by and about Jesus.

The Son (of God)

2. Commentaries should be consulted for fuller treatments of this term in the OT. However, the following need to be kept in mind. It first appears in Exod 4:22 as a reference to Israel—a group: "Israel is my firstborn son." This usage is maintained later: "out of Egypt I called my son" (Hos 11:1).

In between, the expression is applied to an individual—the king (2 Sam 7:14–16; Ps 2:2, 6–7), as God's anointed=messiah/christ. Only in the plural is there a reference to supernatural beings, e.g., members of the divine council: Job 1:6; 2:1; Ps 82:1, 6. One has to wait for the NT to find an explosion of the articular form ("*the* Son of God")—and always with reference to Jesus. For a succinct treatment of this and allied expressions of the Greco-Roman period, see "Savior Gods in the Mediterranean World."[18]

3. So far as "Son of God" is concerned, the following can be said overall. It is the supreme title of confession regarding the identity/status of Jesus. Generally speaking, it is members of the supernatural world who use it, both divine (1:11; 9:7) and demonic (1:24; 3:11; 5:7). Yet, little (if anything) is said about the task/assignment of the Son. While there can be no doubt that Jesus *is* the Son, one does not know what he is to *do* as Son. The single exception might be the destruction of unclean spirits (1:24) and the receiving of crops from the vineyard (12:2, 6). However, the latter belongs to a parabolic representation of Jesus' mission. (See map 21 for a separate analysis of 12:1–12.)

4. Jesus' regular response to this usage is to avoid the term (except in that oblique manner) and to suppress its use in public settings by demons (1:24, where the Greek imperfect indicative conveys the sense of ongoing activity in the past; and 3:11). The lack of such a prohibition at 5:7 can be explained by the private, remote setting in the desert. No one is around to hear. See map 31 for the secrecy phenomena displayed in full and for a suggested solution to the christological aspect of them.

5. Another tack is to shift attention to the Son of Man, as in 9:9 and 14:61, the latter in response to the high priest's interrogation. See map 19 for a more detailed display of the phenomenon of shifting. According to 9:9, when is the secret of Jesus' identity as Son to end? As "high" a Christology as this is throughout the Gospel, does 13:32 suggest limitations—so far as the earthly Son [of God] is concerned?

6. Thus, the Roman (Gentile) executioner's confession (15:39), as the first instance of a human's recognizing Jesus, unaided by supernatural insight, creates a moment of supreme irony. Neither disciple nor Jewish high priest gets to exercise this privilege.

---

18. In Cartlidge and Dungan, *Documents*, 5–16.

The Christ/Messiah

7. Consult commentaries for a fuller treatment of this term, which derives from the Hebrew word meaning "anointed" (*mashiakh*), the Greek being *khristos*. In most instances, it refers to the anointed kings of Judah and Israel, each being God's "messiah" or "christ." In the HB, the absolute form—"*the* Messiah/Christ"—never occurs as the designation for the deliverer of God's people. However, one finds such usage plentiful in the NT—again, in reference to Jesus. Between the Testaments (or, better, during the Second Temple period), messianic expectation took various forms and was expressed with different levels of clarity and intensity.

8. At 1:1, many readers incorrectly assume that "Christ" was Jesus' family name. The next occasion of its appearance is deep in the middle of the gospel (8:29). Yet again, after Peter confesses Jesus' status/identity as the Christ, that information is immediately suppressed (v. 31). What, according to v. 31 is the role which the Messiah is to play? What does Peter's reaction suggest about his (and others') understanding of what the Christ was to do—or not to do?

9. On the lips of Bartimaeus (10:47–48), "Son of David" functions as at least a quasi-messianic expression—which Jesus does not suppress when the blind beggar shouts it out. Nor does Jesus seem to care that he is greeted in messianic categories by the crowds welcoming him into Jerusalem: "Blessed is the one who comes in the name of the Lord! Blessed is the coming kingdom of our ancestor, David!" (11:9–10). How might one explain this apparent change of strategy?

10. A partial answer may lie in the fact that, in Mark's gospel alone, Jesus enters the temple, looks around, and immediately leaves for Bethany (v. 11), thereby pouring cold water on messianic passions. Later, he takes pains to make the point that the Messiah, far from being David's Son, is actually his Lord (12:35).

11. Does 13:23 suggest another reason for Jesus' avoiding the title? Note another example of the shift at v. 26.

12. The high priest's blending of the titles at 14:61 reflects the common joining of them as old as 2 Sam 7:14–16 and Ps 2:2, 6–7.

13. "The King of the Jews," used ironically five of six times by Pilate and contemptuously by religious leaders at the crucifixion, amounts to a messianic category, given the data of #7.

The Son of Man

14. See maps 2 and 3 for the Danielic background to this expression. In contrast to "the Son of God" and "the Christ," this is the supremely narrative term, embracing all phases of Jesus' career—both public and private, beginning, middle, and end. It is never confessed. No one ever says, "You *are* the Son of Man." Jesus alone uses it (true for all of the Gospels). Among the various terms, this one especially indicates what he is to *do*, the point of departure being Daniel 7. The definite article (used with it for the first time in the NT), may function as a mild demonstrative (a point especially associated with Moule)[19]: "If you want to know what *this* son of man is about, go back to *that* son of man in Daniel 7." When others, supernatural or human, use one of the other categories, Jesus shifts to the Son of Man (8:29, 31; 9:7, 9; 13:24, 26; 14:61). What are the implications of this move? Can there be any doubt that this Christology dominates every other one and defines the behavioral role that each is to play?

Lord

15. This is the most varied in usage. In some instances, it is a reference to Israel's God (1:3; 5:19; 11:9; 12:11, 29–30; 13:20). In other cases, an honorific title is in view (of Jesus: 7:28; 10:51; of a master: 12:9; 13:35). A loftier connotation to this term seems to be apparent at 2:28; 11:3; 12:36–37.

Teacher

16. Most surprising is this category, which numerically is the most frequent. In only one case is it absolute: "the Teacher" (5:35). All twelve of the other uses are in the vocative, where Jesus is addressed as "Teacher." (Of these, four are "Rabbi" or "Rabbouni" [9:5; 10:51; 11:21; 14:45].) Only

---

19. Moule, *Origin*, 13.

a single person ever addresses Jesus by his name: blind Bartimaeus (10:47). Demons do so—twice (1:24; 5:7). Of course, it occurs frequently in third person narrative.

Implications

17. Which titles are most commonly used in Christian evangelism and pulpit preaching?

18. Which is not used (or underused)? Why do you think that this is so?

19. What difference would it make if the church's practice were to imitate Jesus' own?

31. The Messianic (and Son of God) Secret in Mark

	A	B	C	D	E	F	G
	Christology Suppressed	Parables Explained: Disciples Alone	Private Teaching to Disciples Alone	Cures Done in Private	Reporting Cures Forbidden	Traveling Incognito	Termination
1	25, 34				44		
2							
3	12						
4		10–20, 33–34					
5				1–13, 37–42	43		
6							
7		17–23		29–30, 33–35	36	24	
8	30	16–21	31–33	22–25	26		
9	9		2–8, 31–50			30	9
10			10–12, 32–45				
11			20–26				
12							
13			full chapter				
14			14–42				61–62

1. In 1901, William (not Wilhelm) Wrede argued that such data (which he regarded as formulaic and therefore historically unreliable), led to the conclusion that Mark's gospel represents stage three in the development

of the early church's belief about Jesus' messiahship—rather than what he himself thought about it. Stage one is reflected at Acts 2:36, where Peter claimed on the Day of Pentecost, in the first Christian sermon, that God had made Jesus both Lord and Christ via the resurrection (See also Rom 1:4.) Stage two is evidenced at Mark 8:30, where Peter confesses Jesus as the Christ before the resurrection. Faced with this contradiction, the Evangelist sought to reconcile the two positions with a narrative wherein Jesus accepted the appellation (with revisions) but urged his followers to keep it secret until the resurrection (9:9). Only thereafter could it be made public. See *Das Messiasgeheimnis in den Evangelien* and the translation by J. C. G. Grieg, *The Messianic Secret*.

2. Wrede's work is regarded as a watershed in gospels study, which heretofore had relied on Mark's as the earliest, most historically reliable account upon which to base biographies of Jesus. Henceforth, scholars either traveled the Wredestrasse, or they took the street paved by Albert Schweitzer. Although the great polymath found Mark and the other Synoptic Gospels to be more reliable historically, his interpretation of the evidence in the light of contemporaneous Jewish eschatology led to a portrayal of an apocalyptically driven Jesus whose vision of the immediate future was crushed by the wheel of history.

3. For a treatment of the trends in scholarship regarding the secrecy/privacy phenomena through the early 70s of the last century, see the introduction to Greig's translation, which appeared a full seventy years after the original. Albert Schweitzer's *The Quest of the Historical Jesus: A Critical Study of Its Progress from Reimarus to Wrede* was translated a mere four years following the publication in 1906 of *Von Reimarus zu Wrede: eine Geschichte der Leben-Jesu-Forschung* [lit.: *From Reimarus to Wrede: A History of Life of Jesus Research*]. The most extensive, recent attempt to solve the riddle of Jesus' reticence is by David F. Watson. See pp. 3–17 for his review of scholarship since Wrede through 2010.

4. I have faulted Wrede for abandoning his own program: to analyze the secrecy phenomena on the basis of the internal evidence of the gospels (principally Mark's). Before completing the project, he had left the terrain of the text in an appeal to external evidence: that of Acts 2:36 and Rom

1:4. In the end, Wrede had mined the gospel and NT accounts for data to construct the history of early Christian religion.[20]

5. If one keeps to the text of Mark as a literary phenomenon, it is possible to argue the following from the narrative itself.[21] The gospel presupposes the long-standing biblical, "bipolar" model for human agency (whether that be sonship or messiahship): status/identity must be complemented/perfected by role/task. The son in nature/being (or by adoption) must behave as such. The one designated as the Lord's anointed must do the work of his messiah/christ. Thus, Jesus kept his identity as God's Son/Messiah secret until his role of obedience (conveyed by "the Son of Man") had been completed at death. Until then, proclaiming the status alone risked telling a half-truth (tantamount to a falsehood). Furthermore, with the possibility of disobedience existing as an option (he prayed three times, "Remove this cup from me" [14:36]), one could not guarantee the outcome. Only when both "poles" of the model were in place (after the one had perfected/completed the other), could his followers announce the full truth about the Son and Messiah—i.e., after the resurrection of the Son of Man (9:9).

6. Of course, such a literary explanation is not the same as an historical reconstruction. Even if my literary proposal is not convincing to the general reader, he or she must still deal with the secrecy phenomena, especially if so many have assumed (or have been taught) that Jesus had gone everywhere publicly declaring his messiahship or sonship—or at least had allowed others to do so.

---

20. Lemcio, *Past of Jesus*, 20–22.
21. Lemcio, "Intention," 198–99; Lemcio, *Past of Jesus*, 45–46.

APPENDIX

"The Elder" on Mark's Gospel

Eusebius. *History of the Church.* III.39.14–15

THE FOLLOWING TRANSLATION OF "the Elder's/Presbyter's" remarks, as recounted by Bp. Papias of Hierapolis (ca. 140 CE) and cited by Eusebius (early to mid-fourth century CE), is found in Schaff, 172–73. Differences among translators and editors do not substantially affect the point that I make in the preface.

> This also the presbyter said: Mark, having become the interpreter of Peter, wrote down accurately, though not indeed in order, whatsoever he remembered of the things said or done by Christ. For he neither heard the Lord nor followed him, but afterward, as I said, he followed Peter, who adapted his teaching to the needs of his hearers, but with no intention of giving a connected account of the Lord's discourses, so that Mark committed no error while he thus wrote some things as he remembered them. For he was careful of one thing, not to omit any of the things he had heard, and not to state any of them falsely.

Bibliography

Bowker, John. "The Son of Man." *JTS* 28/1 (April 1977): 19–48.
Burkett, Delbert. *The Son of Man Debate: A History and Evaluation*. SNTSMS 107. Cambridge: University Press, 1999.
Caird, George B. "The Language of Eschatology." Chap. 14 in *The Language and Imagery of the Bible*. Philadelphia: Westminster, 1980.
Cartlidge, David R., and David Dungan, eds. *Documents for the Study of the Gospels*. 2nd ed. Minneapolis: Fortress, 1994.
Charles, R. H., ed. *Apocrypha and Pseudepigrapha of the Old Testament, Volume Two: Pseudepigrapha*. Oxford: Clarendon, 1913.
Charlesworth, James H., ed. *The Old Testament Pseudepigrapha*. Vol. 2, *Expansions of the Old Testament and Legends, Wisdom and Philosophical Literature, Prayers, Psalms, and Odes, Fragments of Lost Judeo-Hellenistic Works*. New York: Doubleday, 1985.
Collins, John J. *Daniel: A Commentary on the Book of Daniel*. Minneapolis: Fortress, 1993.
Cranfield, C. E. B. *The Gospel According to St. Mark*. Cambridge Greek Testament Commentary. Cambridge: University Press, 1966.
Dittenberger, Wilhelm, ed. *Orientis Graeci Inscriptiones Selectae: Supplementum Sylloges Inscriptionum Graecarum*. 2 vols. Hildesheim: Georg Olms, 1960.
Eusebius of Caesarea. *Eusebius: The Church History from A.D. 1–324, Life of Constantine the Great, Oration in Praise of Constantine*. Nicene and Post-Nicene Fathers 1. Edited by Philip Schaff and Henry Wallace. New York: Cosimo, 2007.
Harvey, Antony E. *Jesus and the Constraints of History*. London: Duckworth, 1982.
Hooker, Morna D. *The Son of Man in Mark*. London: SPCK, 1967.
Kaehler, Martin. *The So-Called Historical Jesus and the Historic Biblical Christ*. Edited by C. Braaten. Philadelphia: Fortress, 1964.
Kee, Howard Clark, ed. *The New Testament in Context: Sources and Documents*. Englewood Cliffs, NJ: Prentice-Hall, 1984.
———, ed. *The Origins of Christianity: Sources and Documents*. Englewood Cliffs, NJ: Prentice-Hall, 1973.
———, transl. "The Testament of Levi" in *The Old Testament Pseudepigrapha: Apocalyptic Literature and Testaments*, edited by J. H. Charlesworth, 1:795. Garden City, NY: Doubleday, 1983.
Kim, Seyoon. *"The 'Son of Man'" as the Son of God*. Grand Rapids: Eerdmans, 1983.
Lemcio, Eugene E. "External Evidence for the Structure and Function of Mark iv. 1–20, vii. 14–23, and viii. 14–21." *JTS* n.s. 29/2 (October 1978): 323–38.
———. "The Intention of the Evangelist, Mark." *NTS* 32/2 (1986): 187–206.
———. *Navigating Revelation: Charts for the Voyage. A Pedagogical Aid*. Eugene, OR: Wipf and Stock, 2011.
———. *The Past of Jesus in the Gospels*. SNTSMS 68. Cambridge: Cambridge University Press, 1991.
———. "'Son of Man,' 'Pitiable Man,' 'Rejected Man': Equivalent Expressions in the Old Greek of Daniel." *TB* 56/1 (2005): 43–60.

Bibliography

Lemcio, Eugene E., and Robert W. Wall. *The New Testament as Canon: A Reader in Canonical Criticism*. Sheffield, UK: Academic Press, 1992.

Moule, C. F. D. *An Idiom Book of New Testament Greek*. 2nd ed. Cambridge: Cambridge University Press, 1963.

———. *The Origin of Christology*. Cambridge: Cambridge University Press, 1977.

Pietersma, Albert, and Benjamin G. Wright, eds. *The New English Translation of the Septuagint* [NETS]. Oxford: Oxford University Press, 2007.

Rowland, Christopher. *The Open Heaven: A Study of Apocalyptic in Judaism and Early Christianity*. New York: Crossroad, 1982.

Schweitzer, Albert. *The Quest of the Historical Jesus: A Critical Study of Its Progress from Reimarus to Wrede*. Translated by W. Montgomery. London: Adam & Charles Black, 1911.

———. *Von Reimarus zu Wrede: eine Geschichte der Leben-Jesu-Forschung*. Tuebingen: Mohr Siebeck, 1906.

Snodgrass, Klyne. *The Parable of the Wicked Tenants: An Inquiry into Parable Interpretation*. WUNT 27. Tuebingen: Mohr Siebeck, 1983.

———. "Recent Research on the Parable of the Wicked Tenants: An Assessment." *BR* 8 (1988): 187–216.

Tolbert, Mary Anne. *Sowing the Gospel: Mark's Work in Literary-Historical Perspective*. Minneapolis: Fortress, 1989.

Traina, Robert A. *Methodical Bible Study: A New Approach to Hermeneutics*. New York: Biblical Seminary in New York, 1952.

Watson, David F. *Honor Among Christians: The Cultural Key to the Messianic Secret*. Minneapolis: Fortress, 2010.

Wrede, William. *Messiasgeheimnis in den Evangelien*. Goettingen: Vandenhoeck and Ruprecht, 1901.

———. *The Messianic Secret*. Translated by J. C. G. Grieg. London: James Clark, 1971.

www.ingramcontent.com/pod-product-compliance
Lightning Source LLC
Chambersburg PA
CBHW070109100426
42743CB00012B/2703